THE HUNGRY DEER

H F CANTRELL

Balboa Press books may be ordered through booksellers or by contacting:

Balboa Press
A Division of Hay House
1663 Liberty Drive
Bloomington, IN 47403
www.balboapress.com
1 (877) 407-4847

Interior Image Credit: H F Cantrell

ISBN: 978-1-9822-5041-6 (sc)
ISBN: 978-1-9822-5042-3 (e)

Print information available on the last page.

Balboa Press rev. date: 07/17/2020

BALBOA.PRESS
A DIVISION OF HAY HOUSE

Image of a wooded area

Deer in the Southeastern part of the United States, known as "white tail deer", generally are found in wooded areas. They are nocturnal animals and rarely seen during daylight hours, except in early morning or late afternoon when they can be seen feeding. The deer spend the daylight hours in the woods seeking shelter from predators, such as hunters or other large animals.

Image of shrubs in a garden

Deer feed on nuts, especially acorns, and plants, such as the leaves and stem of this beautiful Rhododendron. It is not unusual for a plant like this to be eaten to the ground level by deer.

Image of a deer (side view) in a wooded area

One of our favorite places to visit is a friend's cabin in the mountains of North Carolina. The cabin is situated in a wooded area that is it sparsely populated. Occasionally, we see a wild animal early in the morning or late in the afternoon. Sometimes it is a deer, a white squirrel or a bear. That is an exciting experience.

Image of a white squirrel on a rock

Bear sightings in this area is rare. However, another special visitor can be seen around the cabin. This white squirrel comes for food that is put out for the deer and for bird food.

Image of a deer eating corn on a large rock

On a recent visit with our friends, they said, "We have a new experience for you". We said, "What is it"? They told us that a deer has been frequently visiting the big rock where they leave corn kernels for animal food.

Image of a deer on left side of rock

Why was this deer roaming around at noon? We watched the deer for several hours. It kept coming back to the rock where to corn kernels had been poured. We were excited. The deer continued to visit the rock all afternoon, even after dark. It was amazing

Image of a deer on left side of rock eating corn

During the entire visit to this mountain cabin, the deer continued to eat corn throughout the entire day and until late in the evening. Probably also at night.

Image of a deer on right side of rock

This continued for each day of our visit. It was so unusual to observe this feeding pattern of the same deer.

Image of a deer also on right side of rock

The deer seemed comfortable coming to the rock to eat.

Image of a deer eating green leaves

The deer would also eat green leaves from the trees near the rock.

Image of a deer on right side of rock

Another trip to the rock for more corn.

Image of a wooded area with a path

A wooded area leading to a bench where deer and white squirrels were often seen.

Image of a deer drinking water from a pan

The friends we were visiting decided to put a container of water on the rock. The deer soon found the water and drank after eating more corn.

Image of a deer behind the rock eating with water container nearby

The deer continued to eat even though the four of us were watching from a few feet away. Most deer will leave when humans are nearby.

Image of another deer approaching the rock for corn

Then one day we noticed another deer. This deer discovered the corn on the large rock and wanted to eat some corn. The deer was larger and colored darker than the deer that we were watching daily.

Image of the intruder deer almost at the rock

When the "Intruder deer" would get close to the feeding rock, the deer that was feeding many times during the day would get between the deer and the rock to protect the food. The "Intruder deer" would move away and disappear into the woods.

Image of intruder deer behind rock eating corn

Finally, when the deer stood on the rock, we realized the reason she was eating so much corn. She was making milk in order to feed young fawn somewhere in the woods.

Image of a young fawn in grass

This picture shows a fawn in a nest in a protected area nearby.

The mystery of the Hungry Deer was solved. She was eating corn and leaves to make milk for her baby.

Many animals protect their young from predators in nature. It is common to see birds feed their young in the nests until the young fledglings can find food on their own. Both parents of ducks and geese stay with their until they are able to survive on their own The young ducks and geese swim in a line with one parent leading while the other follows with the young swimming in a line between them.

It is interesting how these wild birds and animals have the instinct to care for their young until they can provide for themselves. If you see these wild animals in nature, remember that they survived because of caring parents.

Be thankful for caring parents and birds and animals.

Printed in the United States
By Bookmasters